*Breaking Camp*

# Breaking Camp

POEMS BY

MARGE PIERCY

*Wesleyan University Press*

MIDDLETOWN, CONNECTICUT

Grateful acknowledgment is made to the following magazines, in which some of these poems have appeared: *Carleton Miscellany*, *Chelsea*, *December*, *Epoch*, *Epos*, *The Fiddlehead*, *Hanging Loose*, *Now*, *The Penny Paper*, *Prairie Schooner*, *Shenandoah*, *Things*, *Trace*, and *Transatlantic Review*.

Hardbound: ISBN 0-8195-2039-x

Paperback: ISBN 0-8195-1039-4

Library of Congress Catalog Card Number: 68-16007

Manufactured in the United States of America

First printing February 1968; second printing June 1973

*for Robert*

# Contents

*Breaking Camp*

## Visiting a dead man on a summer day

In flat America, in Chicago,
Graceland cemetery on the German North Side.
Forty feet of Corinthian candle
celebrate Pullman embedded
lonely raisin in a cake of concrete
almost as far below.
The Potter Palmers float
in an island parthenon.
Barons of hogfat, railroads and wheat
are postmarked with angels and lambs.

But the Getty tomb: white, snow patterned
in a triangle of trees
swims dappled with leaf shadow,
sketched light arch within arch
delicate as fingernail moons.

The green doors should not be locked.
Doors of fern and flower should not be shut.
Louis Sullivan, I sit on your grave.
*It is not now good weather for prophets.*
Sun eddies on the steelsmoke air like sinking honey.

On the inner green door of the Getty tomb
(a thighbone's throw from your stone)
a marvel of growing, blooming, thrusting into seed:
how all living wreathe and insinuate
in the circlet of repetition that never repeats:
*ever new birth never rebirth.*
Each tide pool microcosm
from the free spiraling of your hand.

Box that dances,
light tomb of laughter and spores.
Sullivan, you had another five years
when your society would give you work.
Thirty years with want crackling in your hands.
Thirty after years with cities
flowering and turning grey in your beard.

All poets are unemployed nowadays.
My country marches in its sleep.
The past structures a heavy mausoleum
hiding its iron frame in masonry.
Men burn like grass
while armies grow.

Thirty years in the vast rumbling gut
of this society you stormed
to be used, screamed
no louder than any other breaking voice.
The waste of a good man
bleeds the future that's come
in Chicago, in flat America,
where the poor still bleed from the teeth,
housed in sewers and filing cabinets,
where prophets may spit into the wind
till anger sleets their eyes shut,
where this house that dances the seasons
and the braid of all living
and the joy of a man making his new good thing
is strange, irrelevant as a meteor,
in Chicago, in flat America
in this year of our burning.

## The once-in-a-lifetime warehouse sale

Rooms for sale. completely furnished.
repossessed lives. just like new.
balls down. forever to pay.

Rooms where brown fogs skim over weedy pillows,
where trucks fart into the blind window
and roaches prance on the maps of spilt quarrels.
rooms of fruitwood credenzas and lamps in tutus
where mothers touch their eyes with marble hankies.
of piered mirrors masturbating,
of mattresses stuffed with sharks' teeth.
rooms of bald queens whose lost hair
festoons the bulbs like Spanish moss.
baseboards wormy with Schumann and soured loves,
where wrong notes nest hatching spiders' eggs.
precinct house benches dark with the grease of
        fearful buttocks.

They are repossessing lives: try one for size,
you can always trade it in on something better.
Have you seen our rhinestone electric lounge chair?
our pavilion of plastic bluebirds? our tilting glass cage?
Choose, sir or madam, choose now: we have no competition.

## A kid on her way

The kid wanders, dazzled by the crowd
that buzzes in the mirrored plushy hall,
matrons, rapists, fairies: winners all.
The rhythm of the games, now hushed, now loud,
is the catching and slow loosing of the breath.
The tables beckon, pools of sequined hands:
beautiful, your face of light commands.
Deaf to the scarecrow mutter of varied death,
sure her fist of baubles will reverse
the turning drift of hungers, she makes her play.
The croupier rakes her brilliant chips away.
She rises, dazed, to fumble her light purse.
Draw a face on the mirror. Look hard. Blink twice.
A bit more death won't kill you. Try the dice.

### Last scene in the first act

In the wind that ripples over them
she hears the goose grass sigh.
His flesh is prickly as a fir.
Cold, his haste, and shy.

She blames the wind but shivers at
the ending she foresees
and when they rise will force on him
in nagging her unease.

Her mouth smiling toward his kiss
tastes metal of a knife.
His youth cuts her as she takes it,
a green boy's midwife.

Which the lamb and which the tiger
neither knows just yet.
Each lies down in a different bed
to incur a private debt.

## Girl in white

Don't think
because her petal thighs
leap and her slight
breasts flatten
against your chest
that you warm her
alligator mind.
In August
her hand of snow
rests on your back.
Follow her through the mirror.
My wan sister.
Love is a trap
that would tear her
like a rabbit.

### Leaves instead of rice

for Eric and Nancy Lindbloom

Out of a formula
rotted through like old shoeleather,
a public convenience licensed
along with machines that vend gum,
you have fallen into ripeness
thick as honey.

I walk to and fro in bonfire smoke
imagining goldfinch mountains,
cranberry, bittersweet,
salmon and mouth red slopes,
you in maple leaves
joined and healing
appleround.

The ledge of a bald
where a junco begs.
With hands mated you climb
a corduroy logging road
wren grey rock, dense pine
over tree corpses copper with rot
where water rustles
under foot, under stone,
through moss soft as the night.

Though trouble is as sure
as the bones you find
in each other's hands,
though sorrow is rust soon,
though love is quickly trodden
as these leaves,
you have fallen into joy.

Let your eyes and ears
leap like fleas,
let your hands be sedulous
as the tongues of cats,
your words together
sweet and foxy in your mouths
as the juice of wild grapes.

## Girlwatching I

From his table Sol is plucking
girls with comic book breasts
firing left and right.
A sweet-sour taste like yogurt
in their studied pouts.
He could suck their fingers.
Their hearts are vanilla.
He would dissolve
them on his tongue
with a final crunch like cones.
He thinks he would not
even belch.
The young are pretty sandpipers
scooting through twitchy streets.
The old can loll in the sun
with faces tooled to fine leather
and brood simple doodles.
But we are the nasty age.
We are honing ourselves and chopping.
On the young we leave
fingerprints oily and acid
that spoil their snapshots.

## Girlwatching II

Shark clean they nose past
with a wake of bubbles that prick.
Do you dream of nibbling
their waterlily thighs?
The young embrace
with a crushing of bone,
then zip up their skin again.
The young are mirror sleek.
They pass through each other unsplashing
where you or I would be flattened
like a dried skate
hung up for sale.

### How you stare

Your smile is a rubber ball
bouncing twice on each step.
Ah those little loves with zippers.
You stand dreaming,
a centipede on honey,
and lick one foot at a time.

## Noon of the sunbather

The sun struts over the asphalt world
arching his gaudy plumes till the streets smoke
and the city sweats oil under his metal feet.
A woman nude on a rooftop lifts her arms:

"Men have swarmed like ants over my thighs,
held their Sunday picnics of gripe and crumb,
the twitch and nip of all their gristle traffic.
When will my brain pitch like a burning tower?
Lion, come down! explode the city of my bones."

The god stands on the steel blue arch and listens.
Then he strides the hills of igniting air,
straight to the roof he hastens, wings outspread.
In his first breath she blackens and curls like paper.
The limp winds of noon disperse her ashes.

But the ashes dance. Each ashfleck leaps at the sun.

## Dismissal

For pissing on her sofa
and (one week later) spraying on her Danish rug
the lady has had her pumpkin cat
— a hairy please-eyed male marked with bars —
executed, by the appropriate organization.
This cat was beset by fleas
but cherished cheap red tuna and any lap.
His nose was an erogenous zone.
Last summer on the Cape he ran away
and her children yowled through the scrub pine.
He is better off this way, she says.
We all get rid of our retainers
when their love, or loves,
annoy us.

## Lapsed

Never to close again
except between planes
when we match coins of lives.
Your eyes seamed with veins
are restless. Passengers
in a fast car
they flick   flick.
My laugh jars
throat of dust
ripe puffballs
we used to step on
in pirates' woods.

Suppose I pounded the table:
your face is stamped on my sleep.
I grow out of you yet
a split tree that
underground drinks
the same black waters.
if you laughed?
if you yelled Get your harpies
off my nape?
if rising you opened your arms
like cupboard doors?
if you bit me?

Memory's a freakish bank
where embarrassing treasures
still draw interest,
gold and tinsel and radium.
Beneath the table circle

lost names crying
in permanent dusk.

Memory smells
like carefully dried love
where I shelter
inside failure's toughening husk,
where each one labors
secreting the amber
that turns gnats
and midges and stinging flies
into jewels.

### A valley where I don't belong

The first cocks begin clearing the throat of morning —
Who's that walking up on Pettijean mountain? —
rasping their brass cries from outflung necks
as they dig their spurs in the clammy cellar air.
Windows upon the mountain trap the first light.
Their bronze and copper plumage is emerging
from the pool of dusk. Lustily they drill the ear
with a falsetto clangor strident as mustard
raising alarm   I   I   I live   I live!

I stand with a damp wind licking my face
outside this shabby motel where a man snores
who is tiring of me so fast my throat parches
and I twist the hem of my coat thinking of it.

"The rooster, or cock, is a symbol of male sexuality,"
the instructor said, elucidating Herrick.
You stuck me with spiky elbow and matchspurt glance.
We were eighteen: we both were dancers in the woods,
you a white doe leaping with your Brooklyn satyr.
Bones and sap, I rode in the mothering earth
tasting the tough grass and my dear's salty mouth,
open and swept, in a gale of dark feathers.

We owned the poems they taught us, Leda and Europa.
We struck the earth with our heels and it pivoted,
sacred wood of blossoming crab and hanging snake,
wet smoke close to the grass and a rearing sun.

That fruit has fallen. You were burned like a Greek
just before the last solstice, but without games.
I was not there. For a long while I hadn't been.

Now you are my literary ghost.
I with broken suitcase and plump hips, about
to be expelled from this man to whom I'm bound
by the moist cord of want and the skeins of habit,
a hitchhiker in the hinterland of Ozarks.

You hardened to an edge that slashed yourself
while I have eased into flesh and accommodation.
The cry of the mouse shrill and covetous in my fingers,
I cannot keep my hands from anything.
My curiosity has been a long disaster.
I fear myself as once I feared my mother.
Still I know no more inexorable fact
than that thin red leap of bone: I live, I live.
I and my worn symbols see up the sun.

### The miracle

Your ghost last night
wiped from my sleep
as clean as chalk.
I woke. Moon ribbed the floor.
A hand wrote, Quit this mourning.
Driftwood of dreamspar
message torn from
the screams of gulls
told me you
had been born again.

A wasp stands in
heat soggy air
above beige grasses
dry as woodash.
I have lain here so long
my chest
is numb from earth.

Somewhere hair of gauze
eyes of a frightened jay
you are kicking
your shrill new hungers
and sucking watered milk.
Somewhere they are just starting
to tease your arms
with pins.

## The simplification

A rolling tank of man, ramparts of flesh,
a capitalist, a federal reserve of food,
a consumptive disease fed with crane and bucket,
he trundled in a gnatswarm of obscene joke
with his wife slim and grave as a nursing doe
and children ripe at every stage in his globe of home.
Truly a happy fat man is loved and not envied.
Then his luck fell in. A mushroom minded doctor;
sweeping undertow; clash of warlords after
a game and a broken bottle uneyed his daughter.
His wife died slowest, an organ at a time.
He burrowed into work and having no god,
cursed no one. His labors flourished as the light
drained star by star from his world, and the cold settled:
complex useful works like steel limbs.
And he like an ancient wooden trunk is becoming agate.
His face is burnished and dark, eclipsed sun
whose eerie silver mane of corona shimmers.
He is perhaps fatter. His cold touch burns,
and he is reluctant to touch and gentle with words.
Rooms revolve around him into silence.

## S. dead

You were unreasonably kind
three different years
and unasked defended me
in public squabble.
I praised a poem.
Gently drunk, you
gave me it.
I never saw you
again. Three
tooth yellow pages.
The fossil fern tracery
of kindness unearned
as death.

Day like a grey sponge
the car spun out in mud.
My head broke the windshield:
long streamered impact star.
When Robert pulled me out
waking I asked
who he was again, again.
Later I pissed blood and screamed.
I rehearsed your act.

Your face is gone, and now
what will they
do with your poems?
Both poems and cars:
artifacts that move.
Loss of control smashes.
Skill looks organic.

But poems do not
(outside of Gaelic)
kill: or save.

There's nothing
of you here,
only words moving
from anger at waste
from an itch
sorry, self seeking
from bowels and breath
entering a longer arc
than the car that killed you
toward oblivion.

### Sitting like a turtle

My fingers are silted shut.
Slowly, serially I move my leather joints
while my bones chirp. Splinters of bamboo.
My belly is soft and cold with constant fear.
Daily to my door from the Ashmaker
little packages are delivered.
When the buzzer sounds I go into shock.
I unwrap the newspaper. Cracked eardrums,
twisted metal, scraps of stained cloth,
the precise fine bones of hummingbirds.
My voice rattles like a dried pea in a box.

## Sunday evening

On Manhattan Bridge
soiled newspapers lift and close
like swimmers going down.
East River stinks.
My shut eyes see green suns
more potent than
that oily drop
sliding under the towers.
Traffic skirts
a rumpled car with a hole
where the driver's head arrived.
The air is scum
on the stone city.
Blood stalls
like the week end.
In Brooklyn
an old man (your father)
opens the cocks wide
on his dead wife's stove.

## Hallow Eve with spaces for ghosts

The joy of wax teeth
to run masked through crackling bat black streets
a bag on the arm heavy with penny bars,
licorice, popcorn balls, suckers.
I knew that when I was grown out of me into glory,
doors would open every night to a reign of sugar,
into my cupped hands patter of kisses and coins.
When the last porch lights doused at the end of streets
I drifted home with stray glutted skeletons
to count over all I'd asked for and for once got.

The pumpkins and pasteboard bones bore me.
I brush past tinseled children. The night
is low and noisy with a reddish neon glare
yet still a holy night ancient and silly.
My hands itch.
I light a candle and yawn, kicking the table,
but though I wait with meal and honey
no ghosts rise.

Lovers manage without ritual or the worn bits
mumbled over their hairiness damage nothing.
Birth is fat and has rooms.
But the dead sink like water into the ground.
While we are brushing our teeth a friend dies.
A month later someone tells us in a bar.
By the time we believe, everybody is embarrassed.
Then, then, we have to start wearing him out
month after month wearing down
till there's a hole where he used to be in the mind.

My nothings, grey lambs I count on my back,
shriveled sea deep babies, why can't
one night be allowed for adding postscripts,
urgent burrowing footnotes to frozen business?
Help the Poor! Utterly robbed, how could men
pray to their dead? You whom we slip over
our minds occasionally like costumes.
*Don't chip off my mural. Please prune my roses.*

Now it is late and cold. The wind
twiddles leaves into rattling gutter dervishes.
The last lost witch has gone home
complaining of too much popcorn, not enough love.
Put the dolls of the dead back in their box:
they do not know
you have been talking to their faces.

## Landed fish

Danny dead of heart attack,
mid-forties, pretzel thin
just out of the pen for passing bad checks.
He made it as he could
and the world narrowed on him,
aluminum funnel of hot California sky.

In family my mother tells a story.
My uncle is sitting on the front steps,
it is late in the Depression,
my brother has dropped out of school.
Somehow today they got staked and the horses ran.
My uncle sits on the rickety front steps
under wisteria pale blue and littering scent.
I climb in his lap: I say
This is my Uncle Danny, I call him Donald for short,
oh how beautiful he is,
he has green eyes like my pussycat.
A Good Humor man comes jingling and Danny carries me
to buy a green popsicle on a stick,
first ice burning to sweet water on the tongue
in the long Depression
with cornmeal and potatoes and beans in the house to eat.

This story is told by my mother
to show how even at four I was cunning.
Danny's eyes were milky blue-green,
sea colors I had never known, verdigris, birdsheen.
The eyes of my cat were yellow. I was lying
but not for gain, mama. I squirm on his lap,
I am tangling my hands in his fiberglass hair.
The hook is that it pleases him

and that he is beautiful on the steps laughing
with money in the pockets of his desperate George Raft pants.
His eyes flicker like leaves,
his laugh breaks in his throat to pieces of sun.

Three years and he will be drafted and refuse to fight.
He will rot in stockade. He will swing an ax on his foot:
the total dropout who believed in his own luck.
I am still climbing into men's laps
and telling them how beautiful they are.
Green popsicles are still brief and wet and sweet.
Laughing, Danny leaves on the trolley with my brother.
He is feeling lucky, their luck is running
— like smelt, Danny — and is hustled clean
and comes home and will not eat boiled mush.
Late, late the wall by my bed shakes with yelling.

Fish, proud nosed conman, sea eyed tomcat:
you are salted away in the dry expensive California dirt
under a big neon sign shaped like a boomerang
that coaxes Last Chance   Stop Here   Last Chance.

## August

How long can all
stand at impasse?
Not a ripple stirs the grass.
The bee in thick air stalls.
Breath clots my throat.
Not a seed drifts down or petal falls.
The sun embalms
in middle air a mote
static as a bubble trapped in glass.
Silence parches into thirst.
Out of these turgid calms
tornadoes burst.

## August, submerging

Till that time when the late light burns the leaves
against the window where I eat alone
domestic comforts rub against my legs:
my desk, my work, my lamb chop and my silence
but then a current flows in through my hair.

Neon sparks kindle a spastic blaze
in streets that form swift canyons toward meeting.
The day's business runs off. Breasts and thighs
soak in the rising tide and eddy swollen.
Mirrors buoy from the dark my drowning face.

This is weather of sorry mating and sly attack.
The prize I'll haul from an aquarium of smoke,
shark or minnow, already bloats and stinks.
Up from the bottom tomorrow mauled and gashed
I'll come reeking, festooned with dying weed.

But the bracing set of current against my flanks
as filmy electric tentacles brush across:
now, only, I am graceful as falling water.
Season of dog and dogfish. Search no calendars.
I make the climate in which I freeze and burn.

## Night of the bear and polar light

Into the wood black as a child's midnight waking
dropping bits of bread a step at a time.
Trees' grey ankles wade in the flooding moon,
quicksilver drips from cobwebs.
A shrike hammers its iron cry home in my nape.
The shadows knit. I can still go back.
Until in the shaggy cave of bark
the hide and slow heart of the bear's embrace.

The snowbirds sport with my bread in their honed beaks.
Mazes of wrought iron lace invent new paths.
The grass creaks with frost
frost at the marrow,
eyes grey and blinded with frost in the empty woods.
The smoky taste of honey coats my mouth.
I freeze here waiting for the bear's return.

## Exactly how I pursue you

Turn once in this cave of prisms, turn.
Face me. Straw and broken glass like jam on your mouth.
The virginities of mirrors bleed you hollow.
Your spread hands strain the air.
You will not touch me.

Antlered dreams: hoofs drumming.
Moon glutted eyes grey as cataracts
wink from the webbed foot of the bed.
My hair is a net of hooks.
Reluctantly you sink in fearing quicksand.
Your eyes over mine won't shut:
mermaid in brown winds she floats and turns
dune hair and dappled shoulder: I can hold her too.
The gnarled ladder of my spine explodes in petals.
Pink nebulae swarm in my throat. The scent of grapes
although you cannot see me. My fingers
if you listen are white bees.
Sun melts on my tongue. I am shining and dumb.

Scrub pine, scoured air, flakemist on the mouth.
My footsteps are slowly eaten.
My breath whitens from stark boughs.
In the snow cave you crouch
weaving a net of hair to hold yourself
and dream of sugar skulls.

## A few ashes for Sunday morning

Uproot that burning tree of lightning struck veins.
Spine, wither like a paper match.

I'm telling you, this body could bake bread,
heat a house, cure rheumatic pains,
warm at least a bed.

Green wood won't catch
but I held against my belly a green stone
frog colored with remorse and oozing words
pressed to me till the night was fagged and wan.

Reek of charred hair clotting in my lungs.
My teeth are cinders,
cured my lecherous tongue.
Only me burnt, and warmed:
no one.

## Now that I am free

Trees scratch at the sky but can't get in.
In the knotted bole of my chest, what howls
but bad dreams where I run through a tunnel of eye.
Under Orion, the hunter with the wound,
the petrified landscape of his hate.
Shale fields where the sky bleeds frozen rain.
Tundra of salt and glass.

The wind's teeth comb his bones for crickets.
His hands were on my throat: I cut him.
Now I am rooted there.
Small red berries and long thorns.
My hands are claws.

## A cold and married war

Loving you is a warm room
so I remember
how I lived on the moon.
Ash and jagged craters
cold bright place under
a black steel sky.
The stars pierced me
stabbing my secret
aches and itches.
Torture of the witch with needles.
Am I worthy, eyes?
Never. Objects
came out of the silence
bizarre as medals
for unknown services:
chocolate cherries
rolling down from Sinai,
rosebuds pink as
girls' first lipsticks.
When I lay down
head on a rock
the rock
recited tirelessly
as a language record
my sins and errors.

The months bled slowly
out of us.
The landscape went bald.
The cold stayed.
One morning there
were regulations posted.

Where I had not known
boundaries existed,
first hedges, then stakes,
finally barbed wire.
His cock crowed
I know you not,
repent, and other homilies.
My bones knocked.
Chessboard of dead volcanoes.
I had to go.

The only thing to do
with the corpse
was to eat it.

## Visitors with too much baggage

You stand with your arm heavy on your wife
who looks about to cry teeth.
Her hair falls gently. The curve of her neck
appeals. I would like to smile.

I press to my husband.
Guilty as a car salesman, he promotes
the surface commonweal and grinds his teeth.
You beat me with the oak flail of your voice
but we have nothing to exchange.

If there were a cave beyond the mirror
say the neutral bathroom mirror filmed with steam
and we crawled through into that empty house
with bloodshot sky and peasoup streets
what could we say?

All one winter, need clamped in my teeth,
I tried to board you. We traded scarstamps,
snapshots of headstones and bone flutes
till the night bled white and the sun rose,
a blister on the ice rumpled lake.
Sparrows fell with claws curled into hooks.

Now, rival clocks, we glare.
Shall we exchange little fingers, or spit?
If we could begin brandnew with courtesies and guesses
or one die and the other write an elegy
for that imperfect past which hangs false wreaths
on live and curious noses.

## Running toward R.

The night is funnel shaped
pouring narrow and swift before me for a mile.
My coat flaps with haste through squat January streets
where stalling cars groan and heave in the slush.
I enter your room already: spritz of hope.
The gates of your arms close on me.

The seconds knock on hollow wood in my throat,
morse of my steps explaining, urging.
I pound on your door: you are gone to someone else.
I meet myself returning. Icewater steps drip, drip.
I knock again: you sit among ten ivory counselors
who pour into your ear ooze of caution, oil of my perfidies,
cram batting of present comfort. Wait!
I can confess with such nice arrangement
you'll cluck with pity to hear me.

Overhead I stream in a smoke colored wind,
Nike with sail wings blasting ahead.
Under I scurry with glass words scolding in my chest.
What enemy do I race white breathed
who blast my eyes with a blizzard of wish and gravel,
who have only myself to name as master fixer
that I love you and am too late to find it out.

## Thing-song

Jagged intractability
of agate pebble and peony.
Wave on stony wave still measured by pulse but happening.
Red feathers beating in on me.
Not gorget. Not bird. Nor peony.
You once shimmering like a gong in time thing,
let me in for a flash to the stroke of red
as blood's flowering word swells in my head.
Hard says finger, cold says tongue:
pebble and flower unknown but sung.

The sum of knowing/having I can get
wingtip touch of push and hair and wet.
Body on body laboring lies.
Open your opaque and agate eyes
(words mumbled and acted, love and man,
words to wave for whoop and grieve)
that I may press up and receive
what I can.
Distant at my nervetips, exploding within and still above,
in but not of my flesh. My love. My love.

## The shuttle

From one goblet we both drank wine
to share your name:
label over which
my used face
blinks traffic warnings.

I cannot creep like a mite into your ears
or flow through knotted tongues
to swim your blood.
Can't read the brain's telegraphy
in eyes of wavewet pebbles.
Your mouth speaks on my breast
only desire.

Talk to me! Our hot breath
fattens red and gold balloons.
Acrobatic words fly and wheel,
dip, soar and claw in the mutating light.

Side by side we lie
shrouded in sheet and darkness
spouting dreams as
Earth like a silent ferris wheel
bears us under.

The sun bleeds through
membranes of curtain and eyelid.
I sit up to see.
Day by jolt by mend
the meeting of the hands and genitals
a cone of concentrated identity

woven on lax air
that each stitch of breath
I am, you are
still touching
still here.

## Concerning the mathematician

In the livingroom you are someplace else like a cat.
You go fathoms down into abstraction
where the pressure and the cold would squeeze the juice
    from my tissues.
The diving bell of your head descends.
You cut the murk and peer at luminous razorthin creatures
    who peer back,
creatures with eyes and ears sticking out of their backsides
lit up like skyscrapers or planes taking off.
You are at home, you nod, you take notes and pictures.
You surface with a matter-of-fact pout,
obscene and full of questions and shouting for supper.
You talk to me and I get the bends.
Your eyes are bright and curious as robins
and your hands and your chest where I lay my head are warm.

## In wait

White roofs hump
against a perpendicular
sky of slate.
Smoke sags. The Charles
secret, solid,
mimics a field
pigeoncriss, gullcross,
dogtrot over the long tides.
The loud planes cannot
push free, or land.
I keep thinking
the phone rings.
Muffled, locked
love in the mind
packed in silence
moves deafened.
Your name. Your hands.
The tides creep in
under ice.

## Postcard from the garden

I live in an orchard. Confetti of bruised petals.
Scents cascade over the gold furred bees,
over hummingbirds whose throats break light,
whose silver matings glint among the twigs.
Sun drips through those nets to puddle the grass.

If I eat from the wrong tree (whose sign I cannot
guess from bark cuneiform) my plumpness will wither,
the orchard crab and rot, the leaves blow
like cicada wings on dry winds, and dunes bury
the grey upclawing talons of choked trees.

My father was a harrier. My mother a thornbush.
My first seven years I crawled on the underside
of leaves offering at the world with soft tentative horns.

Then with lithe dun body and quick-sorting nose
I crept through a forest of snakegrass, nibbling seeds.
Before the razor shadow streaked for my hole.
With starved shanks and pumping ribs of matchstick
I squeaked my fears and scrabbling, burrowed my hopes.

Seven years a fox, meat on the wind
setting the hot nerve jangling in my throat.
Silence like dew clung to my thick brush.
The splintering lunge. Scorch of blood on my teeth.

Then a pond. Brown and brackish, alkali rimmed.
In drouth a cracked net of fly-tunneled sores.
After rain, brimming and polluted by wading cattle,
sudden swarming claws and bearded larvae.

Now I live in an orchard. My breasts
are vulnerable as ripe apricots and fragrant.
To and fro my bare feet graze on the lawn,
deer sleek with plenty. My hair is loose.

These trees only intrude upon the desert.
There, in crannies and wind scraped crevices,
digging in chaparral, among rock and spine
live all the others I love except my love.

I sit on a rock on the border and call and call
in voice of cricket and coyote, of fox and mouse,
in my voice that the rocks smash back on me.
The wings of the hawk beat overhead as he hovers,
baffled but waiting, on the warm reek of my flesh.

## Interior with sun

Rooms blown in treetop rapids
where the sun floats over our blue bed
borne forward on October
with steampipes clanking.
Pears bronze in a basket,
our comforts ripen.
Surmounting the blaze of leaves
arced dolphins twine, copied
from a fading mosaic
in Delos, among the stones
of a merchant's house.

Love is not a place.
I thrust the windows high,
shove up the rusty screens
so the wind may scatter
leaves waxy as crayons.
Let waste in and ruin.
To fear them will smother us.
It is time to move.

## A married walk in a hot place

A dusty square hemmed by pink stucco
smelling of exhaust, donkey turds and scented oil.
A tough shoves a woman loaded with sticks,
black-shawled, wizened as a dung beetle, into a wall.
He smooths his hair as he ambles.
The bus ends here. Paths go on.
In this landscape always there is someone
trying to break food from the mountains.

We came because winter had numbed us
and a torn man finally froze into the ground.
Two o'clock in hospital corridors, half
past five in the long winding halls of the body,
nights blurring, death rattled and rattled the throat
that had been his, that had been your father.
Marionette of reflexes suspended in cords
running up to bottles, down to machines,
while nurses cooed and doctors told codliver lies.
The blind eyes swerved in the swollen slots.
Legless the fish body flopped flopped
in a net of merciless function: these bones live.
We are animals the tip of a scalpel unselves,
my bony love, hollow with dysentery.

Bulldust floats on the broken road. The brass sky
jangles. Goats' hot amber eyes of rapists.
No shade, but squat by this thorny blistered slope,
your face talon sharp with the habit of question,
block body and a roundness in your arms.
A lizard of green fire tongues a fly.
Predators, we met and set up housekeeping,
bedded now on rocks and potsherds and sage.

The arid heavy whoosh of a raven's flapping
chases his shadow across your pared face.
Sometimes here noon dust wisps are the dead.
On a rim a new war memorial sticks up
toothwhite. Above the joining of three defiles
totter the breached grey battlements of Phyle.
Inside among poppies we eat chicken, talking
old revolution. One standing lintel
gapes at the ravine. When the last man dies
these rocks will turn back to rock.

Only nine in the village died this winter,
the old woman said, offering nuts and sheepsmilk,
giving face of cypress, hands of olivewood,
giving kindness, myth and probably disease.
Twisted by pain I vomit. Then we grip hands
and go scrambling back over Parnes on goatpaths,
you and I, my wary love, eating our death as it eats us,
feeding each other on our living flesh
and thriving on that poison
mouthful by hot mouthful, cold breath by breath.

## The cats of Greece

The cats of Greece have
eyes grey as plague.
Their voices are limpid,
all hunger.
As they dodge in the gutters
their bones clack.
Dogs run from them.
In tavernas they sit
at tableside and
watch you eat.
Their moonpale cries
hurl themselves
against your full spoon.
If you touch one gently
it goes crazy.
Its eyes turn up.
It wraps itself
around your ankle
and purrs a rusty millennium,
you liar,
you tourist.

## Clinic hallway

Six cubicles side by side.
In each the flat bed
of sheeted table,
chair, clothesrack,
receptacle for soiled gloves:
whorehouse parody.

Death is a present hum
like airconditioning.
A nurse pushes a cart
neatly loaded with
paper Dixie cups of faeces:
twenty-four diseases
going past my feet.
I am waiting
for the doctors
to assign mine.

## World problem

I find I am inhabited.
Stupid parasites,
foreigners to my belly,
wetback subversives,
stop mining me.
Cities of my gut,
if I go down
you'll be buried.
A little birth control,
please, to conserve
our mutual body.

But they're laying eggs
in the sanctum
of my appendix.
They're colonizing
the last colonic reaches,
boring the walls
for superbyways.
What do they care?
Wormy centuries fade.
Eroded, polluted,
gradually cooling,
I am their earth.

### Chain of being: something for everyone

The Monarch: a large migratory American butterfly
(*Danaüs plexippus*) that winters in Venezuela.

We hauled from the car
red plums, rye bread and salami to picnic.
Over a stream shaggy in goldenrod
the blue air shimmered and leapt
with Halloween colored Monarchs.
Butterflies, butterflies floated like pollen,
lit like bright leaves on your tousled hair:
kimonos dancing over the scurry of creek.

Climbing the last dune we found the others
who'd crossed Lake Michigan but set down,
too weary for the eighty-foot slope.
Carbonized paper, they blackened the sand.
As they settled to rest (minute/
just a minute) lice swarmed to eat them.
Gutted frames still waved antennae.

We carried a few up to the grass.
We ate our salami by the fluttering stream.
It was very good.

## The writing bug

Succubus despair
squats on the man
who works alone,
rots his sleep,
pecks his bared nape.
He burns his dried nerves
to keep warm.
From his skull flutter
pennons and banners
invisible as the web
in a spider's belly.
Who appointed him?
This mutant social insect,
wasp spitting reams
from his sore jaw
for a paper world,
a mansion so elegant
that the whole noisy
forsaken tribe,
leaving dusty halls,
eggstained closets and
bearing his portrait aloft,
will move right in.

## Lipsky on Ninth Avenue

You look like a mad but polite Odessa angel
lost somewhere off the Cape of Random Fogs.
Perhaps a battleship sank you.
Perhaps you got tired.
Or a boy with a slingshot took you for a stork.
You had a message to deliver that you have forgotten:
prophecy? revelation? revolution? vision?
That is why you are hurrying.
That is why you walk so fast:
you used to have big grey wings like a sea gull.

## Sign

The first white hair coils in my hand,
more wire than down or feather.
Out of the bathroom mirror it glittered at me.
I plucked it, feeling thirty creep in my joints,
and found it silver. It does not melt.

My twentieth birthday lean as glass
spring vacation I stayed in the college town
twanging misery's electric banjo offkey.
I wanted to inject love right into the veins
of my thigh and wake up visible:
to vibrate color
like the minerals in stones under black light.
My best friend went home without loaning me money.
Hunger was all of the time the taste of my mouth.

Now I am ripened and sag a little from my spine.
More than most I have been the same ragged self
in all colors of luck dripping and dry,
yet love has nested in me and gradually eaten
those sense organs I used to feel with.
I have eaten my hunger soft and my ghost grows stronger.

Living in the sun so long my bones are tanned,
I am glad with my love, but everything counts now
and is counted. Gradually I am turning
to chalk, to humus, to pages and pages of paper,
to fine silver wire like something a violin
could be strung with, or somebody strung up,
or current run through: silver truly,
this hair, shiny and purposeful as forceps
if I knew how to use it.

## 1. *Gasman invites the skyscrapers to dance*

Lonely skyscrapers, deserted tombs of business risen
and gone home to the suburbs for the night,
your elevators are forlorn as empty cereal boxes,
your marble paved vestibules and corridors
might as well be solid rock.
Beautiful lean shafts, nobody loves you except pigeons,
nobody is cooking cabbage or instant coffee in your high rooms,
nobody draws moustaches, nobody pisses on your walls,
even your toilet stalls have nothing to report about the flesh.
You could be inhabited by blind white cavefish.
Only the paper lives in its metal drawers humming like bees.

## 2. The skyscrapers of the financial district dance with Gasman

The skyscrapers are dancing by the river,
they are leaping over their reflections
their lightning bright zigzag and beady reflections
jagged and shattered on East River.
With voices shrill as children's whistles they hop
while the safes pop open like corn
and the files come whizzing through the air
to snow on the streets that lie throbbing,
eels copulating in heaps.
Ticker tape hangs in garlands from the wagging streetlamps.
Standard Oil and General Foods have amalgamated
and duPont, Schenley and AT&T lie down together.
It does not matter, don't hope, it does not matter.
In the morning the buildings stand smooth and shaven
        and straight
and all goes on whirring and ticking.
Money is reticulated and stronger than steel or stone or vision,
though sometimes at night
the skyscrapers bow and lean and leap under no moon.

## Kneeling at the pipes

Princely cockroach, inheritor,
I used to stain the kitchen wall with your brothers,
flood you right down the basin.
I squashed you underfoot, making faces.
I repent.
I am relieved to hear somebody
will survive our noises.
Thoughtlessly I judged you dirty
while dropping poisons and freeways and bombs
on the melted landscape.
I want to bribe you
to memorize certain poems.
My generation too craves posterity.
Accept this dish of well aged meat.
In the warrens of our rotting cities
where those small eggs
round as earth wait,
spread the Word.

## The Peaceable Kingdom
A painting by Edward Hicks, 1780 - 1849, hung in the Brooklyn Museum

Creamcheese babies square and downy as bolsters
in nursery clothing nestle among curly lions and lowing cattle,
a wolf of scythe and ashes, a bear smiling in sleep.
The paw of a leopard with spots and eyes of headlights
rests near calf and vanilla child.
In the background under the yellow autumn tree
Indians and settlers sign a fair treaty.
The mist of dream cools the lake.

On the first floor of the museum Indian remains
are artfully displayed. Today is August sixth.
Man eats man with sauces of newsprint.
The vision of that kingdom of satisfaction
where all bellies are round with sweet grasses
blows on my face pleasantly
though I have eaten five of those animals.
We are fat and busy as maggots.

All the rich flat black land,
the wide swirlmarked browngreen rivers,
leafy wheat baking tawny, corn's silky spikes,
sun bright kettles of steel and crackling wires, turn into
infinite shining weapons that scorch the earth.
The pride of our hive
packed into hoards of murderous sleek bombs.

We glitter and spark righteousness.
We are blinding as a new car in the sunshine.
Gasoline rains from our fluffy clouds.
Everywhere our evil froths polluting the waters —

in what stream on what mountain do you miss
the telltale redbrown sludge and rim of suds?

Peace: the word lies like a smooth turd
on the tongues of politicians ordering
the sweet flesh seared on the staring bone.
Guilt is added to the municipal water,
guilt is deposited in the marrow and teeth.
In my name they are stealing from people with nothing
their slim bodies. When did I hire these assassins?

My mild friend no longer paints mysteries of doors and mirrors.
On her walls the screams of burning children coagulate.
The mathematician with his webspangled language
of shadow and substance half spun
sits in an attic playing the flute all summer
for fear of his own brain, for fear that the baroque
arabesque of his joy will be turned to a weapon.
Five P.M. in Brooklyn: night all over my country.
Watch the smoke of guilt drift out of dreams.

When did I hire these killers? one day in anger
in seaslime hatred at the duplicity of flesh?
eating steak in a suave restaurant, did I give the sign?
sweating like a melon in bed, did I murmur consent?
did I contract it in Indiana for a teaching job?
was it something I signed for a passport or a loan?
Now in my name blood burns like oil day and night.

This nation is founded on blood like a city on swamps
yet its dream has been beautiful and sometimes just
that now grows brutal and heavy as a burned out star.

## The 184th Demonstration

This is the 184th Demonstration
the usual crowd
those who try to look respectable
those who don't bother
and those who really are
gee they came too   maybe
we're getting someplace after all.

The police are well trained
and well behaved
although a few comment
on how American they personally are.

Some spectators are offended
by the presence of children
others by clergymen lovers or hair
some stand and clap for us
splinters work into palms
it is hot and we get thirsty
it is cold and we snivel
there are never enough toilets.

Somebody always says, go back to Russia
somebody always yells, Queers
we are well behaved like the police
we march along the allotted route
we sit down where we are supposed to
to hear speakers approved by the committee
when the speakers finish we disperse.

What we do is not beautiful
hurts no one   makes no one desperate

we do not break the panes of safety glass
stretching between people on the street
and the deaths they hire.

Tomorrow is the 185th Demonstration
will you be there?
of course.

## Breaking camp

Now it begins,
the sprays of forsythia against wet brick,
under the sidewalks mud seethes,
the grass is moist and tender in Central Park,
the air smells of ammonia and drains,
cats howl their lean barbed sex.

Now we relinquish winter dreams.
In Thanksgiving snow we stood in my slum kitchen
and saw each other and began and were afraid.
I ran through snow to tell you I was free.
Snow swirled past the mattress on the floorboards,
snow on the bare wedding of our choice.
We drove very fast into a blizzard of fur.

Now we abandon winter hopes,
roasts and laughter of friends in a warm room,
fire and cognac and goose on a platter and baking bread,
cinnamon love under the silken feather quilt,
the meshing of our neat and slippery flesh
while the snow flits like moths around the streetlamps,
while the snow's long hair brushes the pane.

Changeable and violent and honest,
hard head, soft belly and sure in your sex,
stormy and sensible, groper and mapmaker and visionary,
you are rooted in me with pain.
You use me like somebody else's mule.
You are always setting me tasks:
to spoon away a mountain of New York *Times* soaked in Texas oil,
to dam rivers of sewerage with a paper towel,
to feed an army on stew from barbed wire and buttons,

72

to build a city of love on a garbage dump.
I come shuddering from the warm tangles of winter sleep
choosing you compulsively, repetitiously, dumbly as breath.
You will never subside into rest.

The grey Canadian geese and glossy mallards, like arrowheads
are pulled north and beat their powerful wings above the long
        valleys.
Soon we will be sleeping on rocks hard as axes.
Soon I will be setting up camp in gulleys, on moraine
drinking rusty water out of my shoe.

Peace was a winter hope
with down comforters and a wall of books and tawny pears.
You are headed into the iron north of resistance.
I am curing our roast meat to leathery pemmican.
We will lie in the whips of the grass under the wind's blade
fitting our bodies into emblems of stars,
of leaping fish, of waterfalls and morning glories and small death.
We will stumble into the red morning to walk our feet raw.

You go on and I follow, I choose and follow.
The mills of injustice darken the sky with their smoke,
ash floats on the streams.
Soon we will be setting up camp on a plain of nails.
Soon we will be drinking blood out of shattered bone.
The dead will be stacked like bricks.
The suns of power will dance on the black sky
and scorch us to dust.

You belong to me no more than the sun that pounds on my head.
I belong to nothing but my work carried like a prayer rug on my back.
Yet we are always traveling through each other,

we belong to the same story and the same laboring.
You call and I follow, I choose and follow
through all the ragged cycles of build and collapse,
of lunge and defeat,
epicycles on our long journey
toward the north star of your magnetic conscience.

THE WESLEYAN POETRY PROGRAM

*Distinguished contemporary poetry in cloth and paperback editions*

ALAN ANSEN: *Disorderly Houses* (1961)

JOHN ASHBERY: *The Tennis Court Oath* (1962)

ROBERT BAGG: *Madonna of the Cello* (1961)

ROBERT BLY: *Silence in the Snowy Fields* (1962)

TURNER CASSITY: *Watchboy, What of the Night?* (1966)

TRAM COMBS: *saint thomas. poems.* (1965)

DONALD DAVIE: *Events and Wisdoms* (1965); *New and Selected Poems* (1961)

JAMES DICKEY: *Buckdancer's Choice* (1965) [National Book Award in Poetry, 1966]; *Drowning With Others* (1962); *Helmets* (1964)

DAVID FERRY: *On the Way to the Island* (1960)

ROBERT FRANCIS: *The Orb Weaver* (1960)

JOHN HAINES: *Winter News* (1966)

RICHARD HOWARD: *The Damages* (1967); *Quantities* (1962)

BARBARA HOWES: *Light and Dark* (1959)

DAVID IGNATOW: *Figures of the Human* (1964); *Rescue the Dead* (1968); *Say Pardon* (1961)

DONALD JUSTICE: *Night Light* (1967); *The Summer Anniversaries* (1960) [A Lamont Poetry Selection]

CHESTER KALLMAN: *Absent and Present* (1963)

PHILIP LEVINE: *Not This Pig* (1968)

LOU LIPSITZ: *Cold Water* (1967)

JOSEPHINE MILES: *Kinds of Affection* (1967)

VASSAR MILLER: *My Bones Being Wiser* (1963); *Wage War on Silence* (1960)

W. R. MOSES: *Identities* (1965)

DONALD PETERSEN: *The Spectral Boy* (1964)

MARGE PIERCY: *Breaking Camp* (1968)

HYAM PLUTZIK: *Apples from Shinar* (1959)

VERN RUTSALA: *The Window* (1964)

HARVEY SHAPIRO: *Battle Report* (1966)

JON SILKIN: *Poems New and Selected* (1966)

LOUIS SIMPSON: *At the End of the Open Road* (1963) [Pulitzer Prize in Poetry, 1964]; *A Dream of Governors* (1959)

JAMES WRIGHT: *The Branch Will Not Break* (1963); *Saint Judas* (1959)